SILA

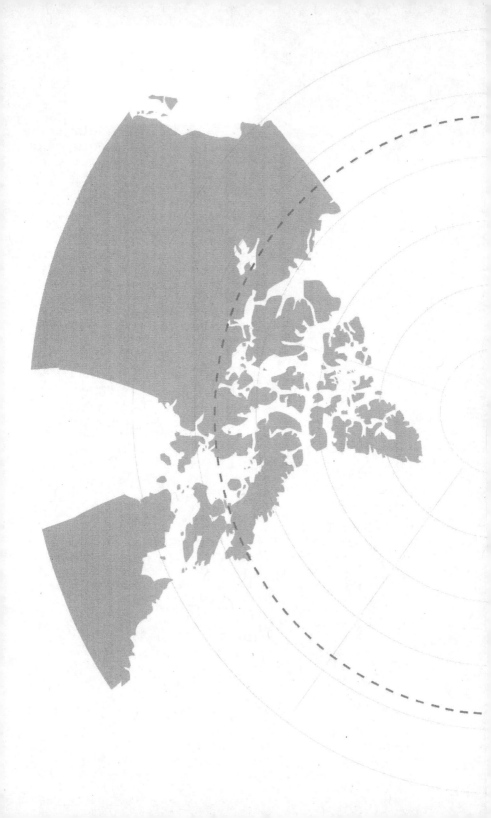

S.ILA

THE ARCTIC CYCLE

A PLAY BY
CHANTAL BILODEAU

INTRODUCTION BY
MEGAN SANDBERG-ZAKIAN

TALONBOOKS

Talonbooks
9259 Shaughnessy Street, Vancouver, British Columbia, Canada V6P 6R4
www.talonbooks.com

Fourth printing: 2024

Typeset in Arno and Arvil
Printed and bound in Canada on 100% post-consumer recycled paper

Cover design by Typesmith
Cover illustration by Lester Smolenski
The Arctic Cycle illustration by Laura Gernon
Series design by Jenn Murray and Typesmith

Talonbooks gratefully acknowledges the financial support of the Canada Council for the Arts, the Government of Canada through the Canada Book Fund, and the Province of British Columbia through the British Columbia Arts Council and the Book Publishing Tax Credit.

Rights to produce *Sila: The Arctic Cycle*, in whole or in part, in any medium by any group, amateur or professional, are retained by the author. Interested persons are requested contact The Arctic Cycle, info@thearcticcycle.org.

LIBRARY AND ARCHIVES CANADA CATALOGUING IN PUBLICATION

Bilodeau, Chantal, 1968–, author
    Sila / Chantal Bilodeau.

The Arctic Cycle consists of eight plays that examine the impact of climate
    change on the eight countries of the Arctic. Sila is the first play.
Issued in print and electronic formats.
Text in English, French, and Inuktitut.
ISBN 978-0-88922-956-3 (SOFTCOVER). – ISBN 978-0-88922-957-0 (EPUB)

    I. Title.

PS8603.I4563S55 2015   C812'.6   C2015-904165-1
                                                  C2015-904166-X

For Michael

The land is like poetry:
it is inexplicably coherent,
it is transcendent in its meaning,
and it has the power to elevate
a consideration of human life.

> – BARRY LOPEZ
> author of *Arctic Dreams*

We must correct the global imbalances
caused by the great disconnections
that have grown between us.

> – SHEILA WATT-CLOUTIER
> Inuit climate change activist and
> author of *The Right to Be Cold*

CANADA

The Arctic Cycle

Sila is the first play of The Arctic Cycle – a series
of eight plays about the impact of climate change
on the eight countries of the Arctic: Canada (*Sila*),
Norway (*Forward*), Sweden, Finland, Greenland,
Iceland, United States of America, and Russia.
For more information: www.thearcticcycle.org.

U.S.A.
ARCTIC OCEAN
RUSSIA
NORTH POLE
GREENLAND
NORWAY
ICELAND
FINLAND
SWEDEN

INTRODUCTION

by Megan Sandberg-Zakian

I had the pleasure of directing the world premiere of *Sila* in 2014 at Underground Railway Theater, a resident company at Central Square Theater (CST) in Cambridge, Massachusetts. In this ambitious and critically important play about our changing climate, the eight characters speak in three different languages, perform spoken-word poetry, travel silently across the arctic landscape, and explain the scientific and political realities of the region in rapid-fire short scenes cutting back and forth between indoor and outdoor locations in Iqaluit, a small city on remote Baffin Island.

Because *Sila* was produced through Catalyst Collaborative@MIT, a partnership between CST and the Massachusetts Institute of Technology dedicated to increasing public understanding of science through theatre, we were charged with crafting a production that made visible not just the metaphor but the scientific reality of climate change. A series of world-class scientific advisers told us the most important things for the public to understand were: (1) We can't get back what we've lost. It's gone. (2) We must adapt to the unavoidable results of climate change.

I knew our production needed to create a space that was simple and pristine enough for the technical information to be communicated effectively, and also beautiful and poetic enough for the impact of loss to be deeply felt on a large scale. The script's inherent themes of interconnectedness and isolation were key, so from the beginning I envisioned a fluid white space that could merge or consume our locations of tundra, living room, Coast Guard office, and ocean. Because I wanted to fill the entire room with shadow and reflective puppetry to achieve underwater and celestial locations, the set essentially had to be one giant projection screen. Scenic designer Szu-Feng Chen gave some structure to sheets of poly-satin by hanging walls of plastic bottles behind them – which when lit from behind created eerie, architectural images reminiscent of ice formations.

And then there were the polar bears – the heart and soul of this play. Audiences have to fall in love with them, but not in a Disneyfied way. They need to be terrifying *and* heartbreaking. I worked with a wonderful puppet design and creation team, David Fichter and Will Cabell, along with a dramaturg, Downing Cless, who provided a wealth of practical information about the behaviour and biomechanics of polar bears. We considered an array of different options, from more abstracted *War Horse*-like puppets, to simpler mask-like elements worn or manipulated by the actors, before arriving at a final design. Based on Inuit soapstone carvings, the puppets were about four fifths the size of actual polar bears, capturing the scale and muscularity, as well as the expressiveness and tenderness, of these impressive animals. I was surprised by how much rehearsal time these massive puppets consumed, but watching audiences wipe away tears at each performance, it was clear to me that the bears were a portal through which we humans are able to access the grief of our changing climate in surprising, profound ways.

Underground Railway Theater is known for its use of puppets, so this approach made sense for us. However, we also did a series of public readings of the play without costumes or props – and I don't think that the story of the polar bear characters was any less impactful without the physical puppets. Studying polar bear behaviour gives you a sense of the grace and intensity of these creatures and the intimacy of their relationships with each other and the land. Actors that are able to capture those elements in their performances can be extremely effective with or without any "bear-like" elements.

Speaking of actors: like any other play, the success of this production was 90 percent casting. I know it looks daunting! After all, the character breakdown has three Inuit characters, two French-speaking Canadian characters, one English-speaking Canadian character, two polar bears, and an Inuit sea goddess. In the Boston area, I'd never met an Inuit person, let alone an Inuit actor, and we did not initially have the budget to bring in actors from out of town – so it was clear that we would not be casting actors who were actually from all (or any) of those cultural backgrounds. Dangerous? Yes. There are so many instances where casting has failed to adequately make the case for a discrepancy between the racial makeup of the actor and the character – such as contemporary productions that employ "red face," casting actors without Native ancestry who are "made up" to look the part. But there are also cases in which a more imaginative strategy for how to represent racial or ethnic differences onstage feels appropriate and respectful. After exploratory conversations with several colleagues of colour, I felt confident that Sila fell into the later category. I decided early on that it was important to cast non-white actors in the Inuit roles, both because of the endemic lack of opportunity for non-white actors in the American theatre, and also because of the very real racial and cultural differences between the Inuit and non-Inuit characters in the play. Since much of the story of the play rests on the relationship between traditional ways of life and the encroaching demands of modern technology and economics, a good local parallel seemed to be found in our own Native community. We did a fair amount of regional outreach as we sought to cast three different readings of the play prior to production. The diversity of our final casting pool was really exciting, including actors with mixed Native backgrounds as well as Philippino, Cambodian, Vietnamese, African American, French, Hispanic, and others.

It is not permissible to ask actors about their ethnicity during an audition process, and for good reason – our business has a history of limiting, not expanding, opportunities for performers based on their race. Knowing this, and also knowing that fostering a culture of open communication around identity was crucial for this production, in which not a single actor in the play would share his or her character's cultural background, I looked for ways to open up a dialogue around race, culture, and representation that would allow performers to volunteer whatever information they felt comfortable sharing about their own background and their connection to the play. The beginning of our casting call stated, in bold type, "Actors with Native American or First Nations backgrounds are especially encouraged to submit," prompting many interesting stories along with headshot submissions. In the audition, I made a point of asking, "What did you think of the play? How do you personally relate to the character?" I'll never forget one performer of Cambodian descent saying that the loss of culture and way of life of the Inuit people felt tragically close to what her own family had experienced.

After casting was completed, I made sure each performer knew why I believed he or she was the best person for the role and that each understood the serious responsibility of embodying those who are not in the room to speak for themselves. My job was to challenge my diverse cast to fully access both our significant dramaturgical resources and their own personal experiences in order to vividly and respectfully bring these characters to life.

Finally, Chantal's beautiful script calls for us to see and feel the titular "*sila*," the Inuktitut word for "the breath that circulates into every living thing." After much trial and error, we achieved our *sila* through a combination of a lighting effect (a puppeteer slowly reflecting a hand-held halogen light off a pile of coloured gel, as if the light itself was breathing) and a recorded soundscape created using the breath of the actors. When this effect filled the room, I could sometimes feel the audience breathing with it. One audience member said in a talkback that she felt we had created a space for collective grieving. I felt that, too. The live space of the performance allowed for us to experience a grief for our planet that, rather than isolating us, connected us and affirmed our inter-relatedness. It's this kind of grieving that helps us to do what the scientists told us we must do: truly accept what we've lost, so that we can find the courage and the energy to act to protect what still remains.

PRODUCTION HISTORY

The professional premiere of *Sila* was presented by Underground
Railway Theater at Central Square Theater in Cambridge, Massa-
chusetts, on April 24, 2014. Produced by Artistic Director Debra
Wise and Executive Director Catherine Carr Kelly, as a project of
Catalyst Collaborative@MIT, the cast and crew were as follows:

KUVAGEEGAI [TULUGAQ]	Jaime Carrillo
LEANNA	Reneltta Arluk
JEAN	Nael Nacer
THOMAS	Robert Murphy
VERONICA/MAMA	Sophorl Ngin
DAUGHTER/NULIAJUK	Theresa Nguyen
RAPHAËL	Danny Bryck
Shadow Puppeteer	Gabrielle Weiler
Bear Puppeteer	Skye Ellis

Director	Megan Sandberg-Zakian
Scenic Designer	Szu-Feng Chen
Costume Designer	Albulena Borovci
Lighting Designer	David Roy
Sound Designer	Emily Auciello
Puppet Designer	David Fichter
Properties Master	Joe Stallone
Master Puppet Builder	Will Cabell
Puppet Builder	Brad Shur, Matthew Woellert, Penny Benson
Co-Puppet Director	Debra Wise
Dialect Coach	Liz Hayes
Dramaturgs	Downing Cless, Alyssa Erin Schmidt
Spoken-Word Poetry	Taqralik Partridge
Stage Manager	Dominique D. Burford
Assistant Stage Manager	Katherine Humbert
Production Crew	Marc Alsina, Matt Breton, Aliza Burr, Chris Demers, Lucas Garrity, Anthony Rhys Jenkins, Thomas Karner, Keefe Kennedy, Kristen Kerrigan, Seth Shaw
Scenic Construction	New England Scenic

Sila was originally commissioned and developed by Moʻolelo Performing Arts Company. It was further developed by Playwrights' Workshop Montréal and is supported in part by a grant from the Canada Council for the Arts.

A developmental production was produced by the University of New Hampshire, Department of Theatre and Dance as part of the Cultural Stages: Woodward International Drama and Dance Initiative.

In 2011, the Consortium for Peace Studies at the University of Calgary awarded *Sila* First Prize in their Uprising National Playwriting Competition: Peace, Politics, and Society. The competition recognizes plays that dynamically engage with social and political issues and/or promotes peace, social justice, and human rights.

In 2012, *Sila* was awarded First Prize in the Earth Matters on Stage Ecodrama Playwrights Festival. The festival celebrates plays that illuminate global and local ecological issues across cultures.

Sila also received the inaugural Woodward International Playwriting Prize from the University of New Hampshire in 2014. The program's aim is to broaden and deepen the understanding of international cultures through a competition for plays addressing relevant themes.

SILA

SETTING

Baffin Island in the territory of Nunavut in the Canadian Arctic.

CHARACTERS

LEANNA (fifties)
Inuk. Climate change activist.

JEAN (forties)
Québécois. Climate scientist with a specialty in sea ice.

THOMAS (forties)
English Canadian. Officer for the Canadian Coast Guard
Marine Communications and Traffic Services.

VERONICA (thirties)
Inuk. Leanna's daughter. Teaches at the high school and
performs spoken-word poetry.

MAMA
An adult polar bear. Played by a puppet or by the same actress
who plays Veronica.

DAUGHTER
A young polar bear cub. Played by a puppet or by an actress.

RAPHAËL (thirties)
Second-generation Québécois. Officer for the Canadian Coast
Guard Marine Communications and Traffic Services.

NULIAJUK
Inuk Goddess of the Ocean and the Underworld. Played by an
oversized puppet or by the same actress who plays Daughter.

TULUGAQ (sixties)
Inuk Elder.

SEA ANIMALS
Played by the company.

PLAYWRIGHT'S NOTES

– There are two distinct Arctics in this play: the Arctic of the Inuit and the Arctic of the Southerners. The Arctic of the Inuit is warm, raw, and fiercely alive. It feels and sounds like the music of Tanya Tagaq. The Arctic of the Southerners is cold, mystical in its foreignness, and rarefied. It feels and sounds like John Luther Adams's album *The Far Country*.

– I imagine the polar bears as large puppets that have to be manipulated by more than one person.

– In the poem "Eskimo Chick," the guttural sound "ahhma" is similar to Inuit throat singing.

– I can provide pronunciation guides and recordings for the Inuktitut and the French.

– Spoken-word poems *Eskimo Chick* and *No Sleep for the Wicked* by Taqralik Partridge used with the kind permission of the author.

– Inuktitut translation by Saimata Manning.

– Inuktitut review by Janet Tamalik McGrath.

INUKTITUT TRANSLATIONS

ACT ONE, SCENE 5

Aingai, Samuel?   Right, Samuel?

Samuel, aggait isaaguk   Samuel, raise your hand.

ACT ONE, SCENE 12

Sananguaqtiujunga   I am a stone sculptor.

ACT TWO, SCENE 3

Tiiturumaviit?   Would you like some tea?

ACT TWO, SCENE 8

Takuqqaujara Inuujaq ullaaq
                         I bumped into little Inuujaq this morning.

Awh, taima   All right, that's enough now.

Makilirit!   Get up!

Paniapik, ajuinnaqqagit   My daughter, I beg you.

GLOSSARY OF INUKTITUT TERMS & PHRASES

Aglu	A seal breathing hole
Anaana (invocation: *Anaanaa*)	Mama
Anirniq	Soul or spirit
Aqsarniit	Northern lights
Iglu	Snow house
Inuit Qaujimajatuqangit	Inuit traditional knowledge
Inuk (plural: *Inuit*)	People (refers to indigenous people who inhabit the Arctic regions of Canada, Greenland, and the United States)
Inuktitut	Language spoken by the Inuit of Northern Canada
Inuujaq	A girl's name (refers to a handcrafted little wooden doll)
Iqaluit	Place of Many Fish (the capital of Nunavut)
Kingulliq	The One Behind (a star in the Orion constellation)
Nanuq	Polar bear
Nanurjuk	Having the Spirit of a Polar Bear (a star in the Orion constellation)

Nik-kuk chips	Dried caribou chips
Nuliajuk	Inuit Goddess of the Ocean and the Underworld
Nunavut	Our land (one of Canada's three territories created through a Land Claim Agreement in 1999)
Paniapik	My daughter
Pitsiaqattautiniq	Respect
Qallunaaq (plural: *qallunaat*)	White man (non-Inuit)
Qajak	Traditional Inuit kayak
Sila	In Inuit cosmology, the primary component of everything that exists
Taissumaniguuq	It was said that in a distant time back (more or less the equivalent of "once upon a time")
Tulugaq	A man's name (refers to the Arctic raven)
Unnukkut	Good evening

ACT ONE

– PROLOGUE –

An eerie twilight. Wind. A sense of limitless space.

Projection (text):
  Listen.

Lights reveal TULUGAQ, *sculpting a piece of soapstone. The wind morphs into a sort of breathing.* TULUGAQ *listens, perfectly attuned to his environment.*

Projection (text):
  Still your thoughts.
  Quiet your mind.
  Listen.

The breathing turns into Inuit throat singing. (Possibly "Force" by Tanya Tagaq.) It is intense, contemporary, unnerving.

Projection (text):
  With some luck.
  Maybe.
  You will find me.

The music screeches to a halt.

- 1 -

A conference. LEANNA stands at a podium.

LEANNA

I come from a place of barren landscapes and infinite skies. I come
from a place of rugged mountains, imperial glaciers, and tundra-
covered permafrost. I come from a place where North is where you
stand and South, everywhere else. Where there are five seasons
and no trees. Where the days last twenty-four hours and the nights
too. I come from a place where skyscrapers are made of ice and
proudly ride winds and currents. I come from a place where the
only crowds are air, sea, and land creatures that gather each year
by the thousands. I come from a place where you can walk onto
the ocean and, if you're lucky, beyond the horizon itself. I come
from a people who have kept accounts of the early days when the
world was rich and urgent and new. When unknown forces lay like
pebbles to be picked by those who stumbled upon them. When
spirits roamed the land like polar bears and muskoxen and caribou.
I come from a world where life and death walk hand in hand like
giggling teenagers. I come from a land whose wisdom reminds us of
our humanity.

This place I come from we call Nunavut. It means "Our Land"
in Inuktitut. It's where we, Inuit, have thrived for more than four
thousand years. It's where we strive to realize our full potential. It's
where we nurture our knowledge of who we are. But Nunavut, our
land, is only as rich as it is cold. And today, most of it is melting.

- 2 -

The coast. Two silhouettes clad in warm winter gear.
One of them is looking through binoculars.

JEAN

Là-bas out by the – out by the pressure ridge. *Tu vois?* A mother
and a cub.

THOMAS

Oh yeah…

JEAN

Extraordinary animals. They can weigh up to fifteen hundred
pounds and travel on ice so thin it wouldn't support a man.

THOMAS

Mean motherfuckers though. One of them attacked a man in
Cape Dorset last year. By the time the search party tracked it down
two hours later, there was no flesh left on the bones. I'm telling
you, one comes within a hundred feet, endangered or not, I'm
shooting it down.

JEAN

They're listed as threatened not endangered.

THOMAS

Whatever. Have you given some thought to our conversation?

JEAN

I can give you the names of other very accomplished –

THOMAS

Jean, they don't need any old scientist who's gonna set up his fancy
instruments and three years later hand them a pile of data the size of
a phone book. They need YOU.

JEAN

I'm busy.

THOMAS

Doing what?

JEAN

One of the last remaining sheets of multi-year ice is predicted to
break away from the coast this summer.

THOMAS

So? Put a graduate student on it. Isn't that what they're for?

JEAN

Plus the environmental assessment is just a marketing ploy.
You know that. They'll look at it and drill anyway.

THOMAS

What happened to you? I don't see you for three years and –

JEAN

I needed a break.

THOMAS

Yeah 'cause now that you're a *Time* Person of the Year, you no longer
have time for –

JEAN

Okay *premièrement* fuck you. And *deuxièmement* I learned my
lesson: science and politics don't mix. And I'm a scientist so let me
focus on the science. Others can do the politics.

Long beat.

THOMAS

How's Liz?

JEAN

We're not in touch anymore.

THOMAS

She still in New York?

JEAN

As far as I know. I think she's getting married again.

THOMAS

That was fast.

JEAN

> Yeah well …

THOMAS

> Ever think about moving back?

JEAN

> To Montréal?

THOMAS

> Be nice to have you in Canada again.

JEAN

> How's Ottawa?

THOMAS

> Thank God I only have to live there six months out of the year.
> (*looking through the binoculars*) You an American yet?

JEAN

> *Résident permanent.*

THOMAS

> You gonna get the citizenship?

JEAN

> *J'sais pas …*

THOMAS

> Tough decision.

> *THOMAS hands the binoculars to JEAN.*

You know, biologists used to think polar bears followed the
movement of ice around the Pole. They'd have the babies in Canada,
raise them in Russia, and breed again in Svalbard or Greenland the
following year. But turns out, polar bears are extremely faithful to
where they come from.

JEAN

They can wander pretty far.

THOMAS

But they always come back. Something to be said about that.

JEAN

I guess.

THOMAS

Makes it clear which territory to fight for.

JEAN

Parce que tu penses que c'est une affaire de territoire?

THOMAS

Yes. It's about national security, control, diplomatic relations, and most of all, money.

JEAN

That sounds like politics.

THOMAS

Somebody's gonna drill, Jean. If it's not us, it'll be the Americans, the Chinese, the Arabs, whoever the fuck, but somebody's gonna drill. There's too much money at stake. If we wanna maintain sovereignty over our Arctic territory, we need to establish a strong presence. Nunavut is huge. It has a very small population: point zero one person per square kilometre to be exact. There's practically no one around to say, "Uh-uh, not here, this is ours." Taking the lead in exploiting our resources is one way to assert sovereignty. Having you, a CANADIAN and one of our most prominent scientists, doing research is another. It shows that we're interested. It shows that we care. And as a bonus, it'll benefit the Inuit. You should think about that.

− 3 −

*A frozen bay. MAMA bear and her young cub
wait by a seal breathing hole. MAMA is still. The
DAUGHTER fidgets, trying to distract herself from
the long wait.*

MAMA

Stay low, *paniapik.*

MAMA gently flattens her DAUGHTER on the ice.

DAUGHTER

Yes, Anaana.

MAMA

The seal sees you. He sees the shadow of your paws moving across
the ice. The seal hears you. He hears the symphony of ice crystals
shifting under your weight. You must learn to be attentive and silent.

They wait.

DAUGHTER

(*whispering*) Anaanaa, how will I know when the seal comes?

MAMA

The bubbles in the water will tell you that he is here. Stay low,
paniapik. Downwind of the *aglu* and low.

*The DAUGHTER looks at MAMA and tries to
imitate her.*

They wait.

After a while, the DAUGHTER starts to fidget again.

DAUGHTER

Why is it taking so long?

MAMA

Shhh …

DAUGHTER

Can we go back to the land and search for something there?

MAMA

The sun is getting higher. The ice won't be here much longer. And when the ice goes, the seal goes. We need seal now while the ice is here so we can wait out the long summer.

DAUGHTER

But Anaana, what if I'm not a good hunter?

MAMA

You are a good hunter, *paniapik*.

DAUGHTER

But Anaana, what if I'm not a good hunter?

MAMA

You will be a good hunter.

DAUGHTER

But Anaanaa, what if I'm not a good hunter?
What if I'm not a good hunter?
What if I'm not a good hunter?

MAMA

It is my duty to make you a good hunter.

DAUGHTER

How good? As good as you?

MAMA

Yes, as good as me. So you may live a long life and be a great *nanuq*.

DAUGHTER

Like the *nanuq* who climbed into the sky?

MAMA

Like the *nanuq* who climbed into the sky.

DAUGHTER

Tell me the story again! …

> *She rubs her head against MAMA's neck.*

Please? …

MAMA

In the early days –

DAUGHTER

No, you have to start with *taissumaniguuq*!

MAMA

Taissumaniguuq … when strange powers were shared among
animals, people, and the land, when all creatures spoke the same
tongue and traded skins with ease, it is said that a great *nanuq*
roamed the land. This *nanuq*, called Nanurjuk –

> *Suddenly, a shift. MAMA sniffs the air at several
> levels then steadies her attention on a fixed point in
> the distance.*

Stay low, *paniapik*. He's coming. He's under the ice.

> *We hear the sound of bubbles rising to the surface
> followed by a tinkle of water. MAMA pounces. The
> DAUGHTER leaps in excitement.*

DAUGHTER

Roar!

> *Beat.*

Where is he? Where is the seal, Anaana?

MAMA

Come. This one wasn't ready for us.

- 4 -

Leanna's house. LEANNA and THOMAS.

LEANNA

No, I'm sorry.

THOMAS

You can take time to think about it.

LEANNA

Thomas, I can't come out and say that publicly.

THOMAS

It's all in the way you frame it, I mean, if you position it so that –

LEANNA

Look, I appreciate what you're trying to do. And I'm not saying I'm personally against it but taking a public stand on this would be political suicide.

THOMAS

Leanna …

LEANNA

I can't in one breath talk about protecting the Arctic and, in the other, lay out a plan for dredging a channel right in the middle of it!

THOMAS

That's not what I'm –

LEANNA

Besides, now that I have the government's attention, I don't want to say anything that might inflame the media.

THOMAS

I don't think having the government's attention is working in your favour. The feds are pretty pissed at you.

LEANNA

Good. Then maybe they'll do something to help.

THOMAS

You do realize that filing that petition with the Inter-American Commission on Human Rights was the equivalent of Canada shitting on its own plate, right?

LEANNA

Don't be gross.

THOMAS

The U.S. is our biggest trade partner.

LEANNA

And one of the biggest emitters. They have to set an example.

THOMAS

I don't disagree. But suing them for a violation of human rights might not be the best way to motivate them.

LEANNA

You don't intend to go public with this project while the Prime Minister is here, do you?

THOMAS

I was thinking about it.

LEANNA

It'll confuse the issue.

THOMAS

The way I see it, if Nunavut wants to address its problems, it needs to develop its economy.

LEANNA

Give me a few months.

THOMAS

I don't have a few months. This is my last season.

LEANNA

What?

THOMAS

My wife granted me ten years. If I don't quit at the end of this year, she's walking out on me.

LEANNA

A few weeks, then.

THOMAS

I'll tell you what. I have a German scientific ship waiting in the bay. It got all the required permits to do seismic testing up in Baffin Bay, but the Hunters and Trappers Association slapped an injunction on it. If you talk to them –

LEANNA

I'll set up a meeting for you.

THOMAS

Great. But as soon as the Prime Minister is back in Ottawa, I'm going public.

LEANNA

Fine.

Beat.

Is this really your last season?

THOMAS

All good things must come to an end.

LEANNA

Who am I going to fight with when you're gone?

THOMAS

You may have to take a break.

LEANNA

Fat chance.

THOMAS

Seriously. At the rate you're going, you're gonna burn out.

LEANNA

Inuit don't burn out. We don't even have a word for that in our language.

THOMAS

Then make sure it stays that way.

– 5 –

Hotel bar. VERONICA *speaks into a microphone.*

VERONICA

Unnukkut ... Good evening ... I'm happy to see there are so many people here tonight ... And so many girls ... *Aingai,* Samuel? ... That's my son. Samuel, *aggait isaaguk* ... There he is. Now all of you ladies can go introduce yourselves afterwards ...

All right ... My favourite way to say Inuit girl is Eskimo Chick. I know that Eskimo is not everybody's favourite word but I think it's a funny word if we use it the right way.

She launches into a spoken-word poem.

Eskimo Chick
you are it
whenever I see you my heart goes
tick tick tick
and then
thump thump thump

and then
ahhma ahhma ahhma
you turn heads wherever you go
you wear cool like only an Eskimo
can, hold the glam
other girls have Louis Vuitton baggage and
Calvin Klein pasts but
you and me
we got sealskin hopes and dreams

your momma musta been a hottie
and she got down and naughty
with some fine Inuk body
cause you are all that and a
bag of *nik-kuk* chips

when we're stuck in a whiteout, lights out, night out
on the town MAELSTROM
you can keep warm with your
quick wits and your
BIG, BEAUTIFUL
mitts

I'll be your compass in the storm

no lie I look you in the eye and see
a fine line of generations to come
all sprung from
your womb – no room
for contemplating suicide
suicide, is not the way to go

remember
I see you
and it's
tick tick tick
and then
thump thump thump
and then
ahhma ahhma ahhma
tick tick tick
and then

thump thump thump
and then
ahhma ahhma ahhma

and you're not just surviving
you're thriving
I hope I'm alive when you're ninety
so I can turn to you and say
Eskimo Chick
you are IT

– 6 –

Leanna's house. LEANNA and VERONICA.
LEANNA waves a letter around.

LEANNA
Here it is! Here it is!

VERONICA
The letter?

LEANNA
I can't believe I'm finally holding it in my hand!

VERONICA
That's the letter from the commission?

LEANNA
This is our future, Veronica.

VERONICA
Open it!

> *LEANNA hesitates.*

Come on, Mom!

> *LEANNA opens the letter.*

What does it say?

LEANNA

>(*reading*) Having completed the study set forth in Article ... I wish
to inform you that it will not be possible –

>*Beat.*

>– that it will not be possible to process your petition at present
because it does not satisfy –

>*She crumples the letter and throws it on the ground.*
>*VERONICA picks it up and reads it silently.*

>A hundred and seventy-five pages of thoroughly researched
scientific facts and first-hand witness testimonies and it doesn't
satisfy their –

VERONICA

>Mom, I'm so sorry ...

LEANNA

>I can't believe this.

VERONICA

>Well, you did say from the beginning that it was gonna be political.

LEANNA

>Of course, it was going to be political. When you accuse a country
of violating human rights, it's nothing BUT political.

VERONICA

>At least, you managed to bring the issue out into the open. That in
itself is a huge accomplishment.

LEANNA

>Not if it doesn't translate into concrete steps.

VERONICA

>Maybe we can address the problem here, in the community. Create
education programs. Invite people to find solutions together.

LEANNA

Let's not have this discussion again.

VERONICA

Why not? If we pool our resources –

LEANNA

Our hunters can't feed their families, Veronica. Our roads and houses are sinking, and our traditional knowledge is becoming obsolete. No number of educational programs is going to fix that.

VERONICA

Oh, so we're just supposed to wait for the government to come and save us? Is that it?

LEANNA

Like I said, let's not have this discussion again. You and I will never agree.

    Beat.

VERONICA

What are you planning to do?

LEANNA

I need to talk to our attorney.

VERONICA

You said you were gonna pull back after the petition.

LEANNA

I said I might consider slowing down.

VERONICA

You said after the petition.

LEANNA

Okay, maybe I said after the petition but this (*indicating the letter*) is not how I thought it was going to play out.

VERONICA sighs.

LEANNA

You don't expect me to give up, do you? At the very least, I need to file an appeal.

VERONICA

I should have enrolled Samuel in a school down South.

LEANNA

What?

VERONICA

In Montréal or Toronto ...

LEANNA

Samuel needs to be here. He needs to be with his people.

VERONICA

Samuel's bored. The school doesn't challenge him enough.
He spends his days in front of the TV, complaining that his teachers and his friends are stupid.

LEANNA

He's a teenager.

VERONICA

And a bright kid who needs something exciting to focus on.

LEANNA

Well, I can tell you a school down South is not the answer.
I KNOW what it's like to be uprooted from your family and culture and –

VERONICA

– "it's incredibly isolating and when you came back, you couldn't even speak your own language." I know, Mom, I know. But I'm not talking about shipping Samuel to a residential school. I'm talking about moving there with him.

Beat.

LEANNA

Don't.

VERONICA

Give me a good reason not to. 'Cause between a father who drinks
himself stupid every night and a grandmother who spends more
time on jets than in her home, Samuel doesn't have much of
a family.

LEANNA

Look, I'll cancel a few trips. I'll take some weekends off. I'll ask
Tulugaq to take us fishing.

VERONICA

You've been saying that for years.

LEANNA

Veronica, meet me halfway here. I've worked too hard on this.
I can't quit now.

VERONICA

You're never gonna quit, Mom. That's what you don't seem to
realize. You're never gonna quit.

- 7 -

*Canadian Coast Guard Marine Communications
and Traffic Services centre. A VHF radio mumbles at
periodic intervals. JEAN with THOMAS, who sits by
an array of screens and computers.*

JEAN

What do you mean cancelled?

THOMAS

Sorry.

JEAN

Ben oui mais ça marche pas de même. I can't – how am I supposed
to transfer to the ice camp if –

THOMAS

The helicopter is grounded for emergency repair.

JEAN

How long?

THOMAS

Couple of weeks. Maybe longer. They have to wait for the parts.

JEAN

Ça pas de crisse de bon sens. J'peux pas – Thomas I'm talking
about a phenomenon of GEOLOGICAL proportions.
Comprends-tu ce que ça veut dire? Someone needs to be there.
Someone needs to witness this multi-year ice collapse and collect
the data. People keep complaining that the models are not accurate
well do you know how you make the models accurate? You make
the models accurate by getting on a helicopter and going where the
shit happens.

RAPHAËL enters.

RAPHAËL

Dude, can you believe this weather? Hottest year on record. And it's
not even summer yet. (to JEAN) Oh, hi.

THOMAS

Raphaël, Jean. Raphaël's our new officer. Jean's an old buddy from
university.

RAPHAËL

Ah oui! T'es venu dans un de mes cours quand j'étais à McGill.

Projection (text):
Oh yeah! You came to one of my classes when I was
at McGill.

[30]

JEAN

Hi.

RAPHAËL

T'es à New York maintenant, non?

Projection (text):

You're in New York now, right?

JEAN

Oui. Columbia University.

RAPHAËL

J'adore New York! Ma blonde pis moi on a passé une fin de semaine là-bas l'année dernière. C'est là que mon fils a été conçu. Right, Thomas?

Projection (text):

I love New York! My girlfriend and I spent a weekend there last year. That's where my son was conceived.

THOMAS

Whatever you say, Raphaël.

RAPHAËL

(*to* JEAN) *Ma blonde est enceinte de huit mois.*

Projection (text):

My girlfriend is eight months pregnant.

JEAN

Félicitations.

Projection (text):

Congratulations.

RAPHAËL

(*to* THOMAS) Hey, you wanna see my son's penis? Marie just posted the ultrasound on her Facebook page.

THOMAS

(*to JEAN*) What is it about the younger generation they feel they have to share every last detail of their private lives?

RAPHAËL

All right, let me grab a coffee across the street and I'm ready to take over. (*to JEAN*) Nice to meet you. Make sure you vote for the right guy in November.

JEAN

I'm not a citizen.

RAPHAËL

Why not?

THOMAS

Don't encourage him, I'm trying to convince him to come back.

RAPHAËL

You gotta commit, man. It's the only way to be in the world. You gotta commit.

> *He exits.*

THOMAS

They get more colourful every year.

JEAN

Come on Thomas. There's gotta be a way to get a helicopter.

THOMAS

Sorry, man. They're all spoken for.

JEAN

Fait que j'fais quoi, là? I sit around and twiddle my thumbs?

THOMAS

Do some research around Iqaluit. We have sea ice too, you know.

> *JEAN sighs.*

Or take the contract. You'll have a helicopter dedicated to you for an entire three years.

JEAN

Sure. In exchange for endorsing the construction of a deep-sea port.

THOMAS

Where did you hear that?

JEAN

What? You thought I wouldn't find out?

THOMAS

Look, what difference does it make? Research is research is research. You still get to collect data and feed it to your model to make better predictions.

JEAN

What happened to science for its own sake? Science to understand the world? Everything has to be APPLIED nowadays. *Ça fait chier.*

THOMAS

The very first freighter crossed the Northwest Passage last summer. You know what that means? That means there will be more. So it'd be nice to have some infrastructure.

JEAN

I told you I don't do politics.

THOMAS

Why? Will you tell me what happened?

JEAN

Nothing. I got divorced.

THOMAS

So? Everybody gets divorced.

JEAN

Thanks for the support.

THOMAS

Jean, come on. Take a stand.

JEAN

I took a stand. I've been taking a stand for FIFTEEN YEARS.
Ç'a donné quoi? A bunch of death threats that's all.

THOMAS

You got death threats?

JEAN

Bon, faut que j'y aille. I've got work to do.

He starts to leave.

THOMAS

By the way, I hope you know there's a community requirement.

JEAN

A what?

THOMAS

Every research project has to involve the community somehow.
New rule from the Nunavut Research Institute.

JEAN

I'm a SCIENTIST. Not a SOCIAL WORKER.

THOMAS

Well, you know what they say. When in Rome …

JEAN

We're in the Arctic.

THOMAS

Exactly. Adapt.

A grey day. Fog. MAMA with DAUGHTER, who fidgets.

DAUGHTER

I'm so hungry … so hungry …

> *She scratches the snow, licks her paws, shifts her weight around, lies down, stands, sits without being able to get comfortable.*

Anaanaa?

> *She starts shaking convulsively.*

(*shouting*) ANAANAA!

> *MAMA enters dragging a piece of fresh meat. She runs to her DAUGHTER.*

MAMA

I'm here, *paniapik.*

DAUGHTER

Why is it so cold?

> *MAMA drags the meat to her DAUGHTER's feet.*

MAMA

Here. Eat.

> *The DAUGHTER sniffs the meat.*

DAUGHTER

It's not seal.

> *MAMA nudges the meat toward her.*

MAMA

Eat. It will give you strength.

DAUGHTER
What is it?

MAMA
It's meat. Meat I got for you.

> The DAUGHTER *tries a bite. She gags and spits it*
> *out.*

Paniapik, please ...

DAUGHTER
I can't, Anaana. It's too disgusting.

> The DAUGHTER *slumps down and hides her face*
> *under her paw.* MAMA *wraps herself around her,*
> *protectively.*

– 9 –

> *The high school in Iqaluit. A hand-painted banner*
> *reads "Environmental Awareness Day."* VERONICA
> *stares at* JEAN, *confused.*

VERONICA
A presentation?

JEAN
To the students.

VERONICA
What's your name again?

JEAN
Jean. Lefèvre.

VERONICA
And you're –

JEAN

A climate researcher. Well trying to be.

VERONICA

Were you asked by one of the other teachers?

JEAN

Non, non it was uh … I'm a friend of Leanna and she –

VERONICA

You know my mother?

JEAN

I helped her with her petition a few years ago … She said uh *elle m'a dit que vous aviez besoin de quelqu'un pour* – (*gesturing toward the banner*) to talk to the students.

VERONICA

My mother asked you to –

JEAN

I'm stuck in Iqaluit for a couple of days and I mentioned that –

VERONICA

What did she say exactly?

JEAN

She uh … She said you were trying to raise awareness about –

VERONICA

Did she tell you she was the one who was supposed to be here?

Beat.

She didn't.

JEAN

She was in a hurry. I caught her just as she was leaving for the airport.

VERONICA

Oh. Where's she going this time?

JEAN

J'me souviens pas trop ... I think it was Vancouver.
Or maybe Seattle.

VERONICA

That's just like her. I organized this event around her. I planned this
whole day so students would get to know her and her work. And
she doesn't even show up.

JEAN

I'm sure she ... Maybe she forgot or –

VERONICA

Don't make excuses for her.

> *Uncomfortable beat.*

> *VERONICA examines JEAN from head to toes.*

Jean, you said, right?

JEAN

Uh *oui.* (*extending his hand*) Nice to meet you.

> *They shake hands.*

I heard nice things about –

VERONICA

Is this your first time on Baffin?

JEAN

Non, pas du tout. I've been coming here for fifteen years.

VERONICA

Impressive.

JEAN

It's my job.

VERONICA

In fifteen years, you must have learned some Inuktitut.

JEAN

Not – I mean I'd love to but *la façon dont les choses fonctionnent* most of the time we're in the field and you know … we have a lot to accomplish in a very short period so there's really no time to –

VERONICA

Typical *qallunaaq.*

JEAN

It's just how science works.

VERONICA

Fifteen years and not a single word?

JEAN

Ben j'sais pas là …

VERONICA

What about *nanuq*?

JEAN

Sure. *Nanuq* of the North.

VERONICA

Qajaq.

JEAN

(*trying to repeat*) Rrrra … Oh! Kayak right? I didn't realize that was –

VERONICA

Iglu …

JEAN

Okay I guess I know more than I thought.

VERONICA

Colonialism has a sneaky way of leaving its traces. *Qallunaat* got the land but Inuit managed to infiltrate the language.

She hands him a flyer.

I write spoken-word poetry. Come and see me sometime. You might learn something.

JEAN

Sure. I uh I'll try.

She waits for him to leave. He doesn't.

VERONICA

Anything else?

JEAN

Well ... I thought I'd ... (*gesturing toward the banner*)

VERONICA

No, thank you.

JEAN

It's really not – I'm happy to. I have to do it anyway.

VERONICA

Have to?

JEAN

Ça fait partie de – The Nunavut Research Institute requires that –

VERONICA

Oh. You're here to fulfill your requirement with the Natives so you can get your research licence.

JEAN

Non. I mean yes in a way but –

VERONICA

You know, Jean, things have changed over the last fifteen years. If you want to work in Nunavut, it's not enough to talk AT us anymore. You have to talk WITH us. That's just *pitsiaqattautiniq.*

JEAN

I have no idea what that means.

VERONICA

You're a smart man. Figure it out.

She exits.

– 10 –

Out on the ice. A brilliant and benevolent moon dominates the landscape. Friendly growling and laughter. MAMA and her DAUGHTER play-fight.

DAUGHTER

I was good, right Anaana?

MAMA

You were very good.

DAUGHTER

I stayed low like you said. And I didn't make a sound.

MAMA

You were as silent as a rock.

DAUGHTER

And I waited and waited and waited ... How long did I wait?

MAMA

For as long as it takes the goose to travel to its summer ground.

DAUGHTER

Longer!

MAMA

For as long as it takes the river to grow into an ocean.

DAUGHTER

Longer!

MAMA

For as long as it takes the glacier to crawl down the rocky cliff.

DAUGHTER

Yes! And when I saw the bubbles, I pounced!

MAMA

You're a very good hunter, *paniapik*.

DAUGHTER

I'm a good hunter.

MAMA

I'm proud of you.

> *They look up at the stars as the DAUGHTER revels in that thought.*

DAUGHTER

Look! There's Nanurjuk, the *nanuq* who climbed into the sky!

MAMA

Uh-huh. And do you see the hunters chasing after her?

DAUGHTER

Yes. One, two, three.

MAMA

And …?

DAUGHTER

And in the back is *Kingulliq*, the fourth hunter who dropped his mitt and went back to retrieve it.

MAMA

That's right.

DAUGHTER

I'm sad for Nanurjuk … It must be lonely running across the sky like that every night.

MAMA

The only creatures who are lonely are the ones who forget about *sila.*

DAUGHTER

How do you mean, Anaana?

MAMA

All life is breath. From the original breath that gave us the miracle of Creation to the world itself, *sila* wraps all around us.

The DAUGHTER looks around.

DAUGHTER

The sky is *sila*?

MAMA nods.

The wind is *sila*?

MAMA nods.

The land, the ice, the ocean?

MAMA nods.

MAMA

And *sila* also moves in and out of our lungs.

MAMA breathes.

See? That's *sila*. And with each breath, *sila* reminds us that we are never alone. Each and every one of us is connected to every other living creature.

The DAUGHTER breathes.

But *sila*'s gift is not ours to keep. We may use our breath while we roam the land but we must surrender it once we pass from the land. Creatures who are lonely are the ones who hold on to their breath as if it were theirs and theirs alone.

Beat.

One day, you will leave me, *paniapik.*

DAUGHTER

That's not true.

MAMA

One day, it will be time for you to go into the world and meet your own destiny.

DAUGHTER

I won't leave you, Anaanaa.

MAMA

And I won't be sad and you won't be sad because *sila* will reach across the land and bring us the sweet scent of each other's happiness.

*The sound of a snowmobile fades in, growing louder
as it gets closer.*

DAUGHTER

What's that?

Suddenly, silence. They scan the horizon. Gunshot.

MAMA
Run!

The DAUGHTER hesitates. Another gunshot.

Quick, run!

They run away.

- 11 -

Coast Guard centre. RAPHAËL is on the phone.

RAPHAËL
*Qu'est-ce que la sage-femme a dit? ... Super. J'peux lui dire
bonjour? ... Oui, mets le téléphone sur ton ventre ... Allô, bébé.
C'est papa ... Pour vrai? Il donne des coups de pied? ... C'est mon
garçon ça – prêt pour la randonnée! ... Oui, j'ai commencé à le
lire. J'pratique à tous les soirs, écoute ...*

> *Projection (text):*
> What did the midwife say? ... Great. Can I say hi to
> him? ... Yeah, put the phone on your belly ... Hi,
> baby ... It's your dad ... Really? He's kicking? ... That's my
> boy – eager to hit the trail! ... Yeah, I've started reading it.
> I practise every night, listen ...

Breathes rhythmically like a woman giving birth.

Pas mal, han? ... Moi aussi, j't'aime ...

> *Projection (text):*
> Not bad, huh? ... I love you too ...

THOMAS enters.

THOMAS
Moi aussi, je t'aime.

> *Projection (text):*
> I love you too.

RAPHAËL

Marie, je t'appelle plus tard.

> *Projection (text):*
> Marie, I'll call you later.

He hangs up.

THOMAS

You gotta tone it down, man. You're making the rest of us look bad.

RAPHAËL

Shut up.

THOMAS

What did I miss? Two Brits still alive?

RAPHAËL

Alive and rowing. According to the blog, they're halfway down the Mackenzie.

THOMAS

Crazy.

RAPHAËL

Nah, come on. Crossing the Northwest Passage in a rowboat?

THOMAS

That's what I said. Crazy.

RAPHAËL

Be freaking awesome …

THOMAS

I see the *Polaria* left the bay?

RAPHAËL

Left this morning without making radio contact. I have a call out to the Ministry of Foreign Affairs. They said to sit tight until they talk to Germany.

THOMAS

Who told you to do that?

RAPHAËL

Well ... They don't have permission to enter farther into Canadian waters. I thought –

THOMAS

Raphaël, you're not paid to think, you're paid to execute. So the next time you have the impulse to do something stupid, do me a favour: don't.

RAPHAËL

But –

THOMAS

Besides, the injunction is about to be lifted.

RAPHAËL

The Hunters and Trappers Association gave up?

THOMAS

The effects of seismic surveys on marine life have been studied for decades. There's no proof that they do any harm.

RAPHAËL

Sure. Firing air guns into the water every ten to fifteen seconds is a totally benign activity. And getting money from Natural Resources Canada doesn't at all mean that this vessel is looking for oil.

THOMAS

Their mandate is to map the sea floor. They're not responsible for what people do with that information. Get me Foreign Affairs.

> RAPHAËL dials the number and hands the phone to Thomas.

(*to phone*) Hi, this is Thomas in Iqaluit. Is John around? ... Yeah, I'll wait. (*to RAPHAËL*) This is important. The data the *Polaria* will provide can help us get more resources.

RAPHAËL

New icebreakers?

THOMAS

Nevermind icebreakers. What I'm going after is a port.

RAPHAËL

A port?

THOMAS

A state-of-the-art, environmentally responsible, military and civilian loading and refuelling station.

RAPHAËL

And where are you gonna put that port? In Hyperborea?

THOMAS

Where?

RAPHAËL

Hyperborea … The place in Greek mythology where –

THOMAS

I swear, some days I feel like the head office sent us some sissy English Lit major instead of –

RAPHAËL

Actually, I majored in environmental –

THOMAS

ANYWAY. (*to phone*) Yeah, I'm still holding. (*to* RAPHAËL) Have you ironed your uniform?

RAPHAËL

Why?

THOMAS

Prime Minister's visit.

RAPHAËL

I don't have an ironing board.

THOMAS

You can borrow mine.

RAPHAËL

I'm not wearing the uniform. I hate the uniform.

THOMAS

Raphaël, this is not prom. I'm not your date asking you to wear something NICE. This is the Coast Guard and I, your superior, am ORDERING you to WEAR YOUR UNIFORM. You got it? (*to phone*) John. How are you? ... Yeah, same here ... No, I'm actually calling to do a bit of damage control ...

– 12 –

Hotel restaurant. We hear the faint noise of diners in the background. JEAN sits at a table, sipping coffee and working through some files.

TULUGAQ enters. He approaches JEAN and shows him a polar bear sculpture.

JEAN

Non merci.

TULUGAQ silently insists.

I'm sorry I'm not –

TULUGAQ puts the sculpture on the table.

TULUGAQ

Just look.

JEAN looks at the sculpture.

JEAN

It's uh … it's very nice.

TULUGAQ

Yes.

JEAN

You're the artist?

TULUGAQ

Sanannguaqtiujunga.

JEAN

Ah. And this (*indicating the sculpture*) is –

TULUGAQ

Soapstone becoming polar bear. And polar bear can protect you.

JEAN examines the sculpture more closely.

JEAN

You think I need protection?

TULUGAQ

Everybody needs protection.

JEAN

Then maybe you should keep it. So it protects you.

TULUGAQ

I am a hunter. I know how to protect. You, no. Two hundred dollars.

JEAN

You're a hunter.

TULUGAQ

Tulugaq, yes.

JEAN

Oh you're *je m'excuse, je vous avais pas* – I'm Jean. Thank you
for coming.

JEAN motions to the chair. TULUGAQ doesn't sit.

So uh ... the Institute said you've worked with scientists before.
(*pause*) Basically I need a skidoo with a trailer to carry the
equipment and I'll need you to watch for polar bears while we're
out on the ice. I'm also gonna count on you to show me the safest
route of course because I'm not used to – *c'est pas mon secteur,
je travaille plutôt dans le Grand Nord* but we had equipment
failure and I'm stuck here waiting for the – Anyway I want to deploy
some CTD sensors to take measurements of ice thickness you know
stuff like that that's useful to plug into a model and can justify the
funds I was granted for this trip.

Silence.

Does that uh ... Does that sound good?

TULUGAQ turns around to leave.

Wait!

TULUGAQ doesn't stop.

I fully intend to pay you if that's the issue and I can also –

TULUGAQ steps outside. JEAN follows him.

– I can also hire an interpreter I mean not that your English – but
you know if that would make you feel more –

TULUGAQ points at the sky.

TULUGAQ

How do you call this?

JEAN

Northern lights. *Aurores boréales.*

TULUGAQ

    We call them *aqsarniit.*

JEAN

    (*mispronouncing*) *Aqsarniit.*

TULUGAQ

    Aqsarniit.

JEAN

    (*a little better*) *Aqsarniit.*

TULUGAQ

    Very dangerous.

JEAN

    They are?

TULUGAQ

    If you don't wear a hat, *aqsarniit* cut off your head.

        TULUGAQ is dead serious. JEAN puts on his hat
        and TULUGAQ laughs.

    We tell Inuit children: *aqsarniit* cut off their heads and play soccer
with it. And if you do like this –

    He whistles.

They come closer. See?

    They take turns whistling.

That is *Inuit qaujimajatuqangit.* Inuit traditional knowledge. Old
learning about living in peace with people, animals, nature. Arctic is
not just numbers. Arctic is stories. Like *aqsarniit* story. *Qallunaat*
learning: lots of numbers. But it comes here – (*pointing to his
head*). Only here. Not good for us. *Inuit qaujimajatuqangit* comes
here – (*pointing to his head*), here – (*pointing to his heart*),
and here – (*moving hands and feet*). *Inuit qaujimajatuqangit* is
alive. Observation, experience. Always changing. Numbers are not
enough. We need stories. You understand?

JEAN

> I think so.

>> *Silence as they become bathed in green light.*
>> *TULUGAQ hands the sculpted bear to JEAN.*

> *Merci.*

TULUGAQ

> Two hundred dollars.

JEAN

> Oh right.

>> *JEAN pays TULUGAQ, who pockets the money and*
>> *starts to leave.*

> So uh does that mean are you taking the job?

TULUGAQ

> I collaborate.

JEAN

> Yes of course that's what I mean. When can we start?

TULUGAQ

> When the time is right.

>> *He exits.*

– 13 –

>> *Eerie sounds of cracking sea ice followed by the*
>> *howling of a rising wind.*

>> *MAMA sleeps, huddled against a snowdrift. The*
>> *DAUGHTER plays nearby, standing on her hind legs*
>> *and acting menacing. MAMA wakes up.*

DAUGHTER

Anaanaa, Anaanaa, look!

> The DAUGHTER does her best "mean bear" act.

Are you scared?

MAMA

We're drifting.

> MAMA gets up and discovers the edge of what is now
> a drifting ice floe.

The ice broke. The wind is pushing us out.

DAUGHTER

Who broke the ice, Anaana?
Who broke it?
Who broke it?
Was it the human who tried to kill us? He didn't look very
dangerous. I bet I could kill him with one swipe of the paw.

> MAMA scans the horizon and tries to assess the
> situation.

DAUGHTER

Anaanaa?

MAMA

WHAT!!

> The DAUGHTER cowers back.

> MAMA takes a moment to regain her calm.

What is it, *paniapik*?

> The DAUGHTER shakes her head no.

Tell me.

DAUGHTER

Did the human break the ice?

MAMA

The ice broke because Nuliajuk is angry. And Nuliajuk is angry because humans have angered her.

DAUGHTER

Nuliajuk in the ocean?

MAMA

Yes, Nuliajuk in the ocean.

DAUGHTER

Oh.

The DAUGHTER peers into the water, frightened.

MAMA

We need to swim back to shore before the wind pushes us farther out. Can you do that?

DAUGHTER

It's a long way.

MAMA

But you're a good swimmer. And nothing can happen to you because I'm the strongest *nanuq* in the world, remember?

The DAUGHTER nods.

You stay close.

DAUGHTER

Yes, Anaana.

They lower themselves into the water and swim away.

Leanna's house. LEANNA and VERONICA.

VERONICA

Mom, you promised!

LEANNA

I'm trying, honey. Honest to God, I fully intend to be more present but you know how it is, sometimes I don't find out until the very last minute.

LEANNA picks up the phone and listens for a dial tone.

Don't tell me the line is dead again.

VERONICA

I just can't get over the fact that you stood me up.

LEANNA

Was it like that this morning?

She tries unplugging and replugging the phone, turning it on and off, and so on.

VERONICA

I promised the students an exciting day with one of the most important leaders in their community and you didn't even show up! There's no excuse for that.

LEANNA slams the phone.

LEANNA

Why can't we get a reliable phone line in this town? You'd think that for what we pay, we could expect the service to WORK.

VERONICA

Mom ...

LEANNA

Look, I know you're angry with me but –

LEANNA checks her watch.

VERONICA

I need your help …

LEANNA

I'm about to be interviewed live for a CBC news program. By the way, do you know that since we filed the appeal, my speaking engagements have quadrupled? One of our neighbours must have a satellite phone.

VERONICA

Samuel got caught stealing gas yesterday.

LEANNA

Oh.

VERONICA

He and two of his friends. They were heading toward the pit at the end of the Road to Nowhere. I think they were gonna sniff it.

Beat.

LEANNA

Look, I – Let me just make this call, okay?

VERONICA

And then what?

LEANNA

And then we'll talk about it.

LEANNA listens for the dial tone again.

Ah! It's working!

She starts to dial. VERONICA snatches up the phone.

Veronica, don't.

VERONICA

Mom, MY SON, YOUR GRANDSON, may be inhaling gasoline.
Can you take that in? Can you let that information reach the part of
you that is still capable of a normal emotional response?

LEANNA

Veronica, DO NOT PATRONIZE ME!

VERONICA

You're going on and on about a stupid call with some stupid
radio station while I'm here, doing everything I can to hold this
family together. Your GRANDSON, Mom! Isn't that more
important than –

LEANNA

Yes, it's important! Why do you think I'm so frantic all the time?
I spend my days trying to figure out how to influence policies so
Samuel doesn't become another statistic. He's the reason I get up in
the morning. He's what keeps me awake at night. He's why I believe
the issues we're facing need to be addressed NOW. Now give me
the phone.

VERONICA

I've applied for a teaching position in Montréal.

LEANNA

Oh, would you stop it with that ridiculous idea –

VERONICA

RIDICULOUS?

LEANNA

– and give me the goddamn phone!

LEANNA tries to grab the phone.

VERONICA

If the South was good enough for you –

LEANNA

Give it to me!

VERONICA

– why wouldn't it be good enough for us? I mean it's not like you
rushed back here after –

*The phone rings. The two women look at it,
surprised.*

Hello? ... Yes, this is Samuel's mother ... Why? Where is
he? ... Where is he? ...

*She freezes. The blood drains from her face. She looks
at LEANNA.*

LEANNA

What? What happened?

LEANNA grabs the phone.

Hello?

VERONICA remains glued in her spot, expressionless.

- 15 -

*Heavy panting. The open sea. MAMA tries to prop up
her exhausted DAUGHTER on a small iceberg.*

MAMA

There ... That's good ... Rest for a little bit ...

*The DAUGHTER is too heavy. The iceberg rolls over,
throwing her back into the water.*

DAUGHTER

Anaanaa!

MAMA

Don't worry, I have you … Climb on my back.

As best she can, the DAUGHTER climbs on MAMA's back.

MAMA

Now, hold tight. We're not very far. I'll get you there.

MAMA swims.

The DAUGHTER's panting gradually slows as the Earth's breathing rises.

MAMA swims.

Soon, the DAUGHTER and the Earth breathe in unison, their breathing rising up and down with the swell of the ocean.

MAMA swims.

It's beautiful. Calm. A moment of perfect harmony.

Then as the DAUGHTER's breath starts to fade, long strands of something – plants perhaps – emerge from the water.

MAMA

Hold on … We're very close …

The strands wrap themselves around the DAUGHTER.

MAMA desperately swims toward the approaching shore.

The DAUGHTER, all entangled now, slides off MAMA's back. She sinks into the water as the sea swallows her breath in one swooping motion.

MAMA

Paniapik!

> *MAMA dives. She grabs her sinking DAUGHTER by the scruff of the neck and tries to pull her up.*
>
> *More strands appear and fight back. There is a violent tug-of-war until MAMA loses her grip. The strands quickly envelop the DAUGHTER and drag her to the bottom of the ocean.*
>
> *MAMA climbs onto firm ground and runs up and down the shore, peering into the water.*

MAMA

Paniapik! ... Paniapik! ...

> *The DAUGHTER is nowhere to be found.*
>
> *MAMA lets out a series of long desperate wails.*

MAMA

(*softly*) *Paniapik ...*

– END OF ACT ONE –

ACT TWO

– 1 –

Commission hearing. LEANNA stands at a podium.

LEANNA

Mr. Chairman, members of the Appeal Board … Thank you for this opportunity to speak before the Inter-American Commission on Human Rights in defence of our petition against the United States.

As we all know, average temperatures in the Arctic are rising twice as fast as in the rest of the world. Industrialized countries that do not recognize this and take action to reduce their emissions violate our basic human rights to life, health, culture, and –

Beat.

She looks at the audience.

Actually …

She tosses her notes aside.

The real issue is not climate change … How warm, how cold … how much water, how much ice … what animal species will make it, and what islands won't … No. The real issue has to do with something much more fundamental: our own humanity … So you may tell me that the world's economic survival is more important than the well-being of a small Arctic nation. You may tell me that anxiety and fear and depression are a matter of personal choice, not of environmental stewardship. You may tell me that drug abuse and … teenage suicide …

Beat as she fights back tears.

… are by no means a sign of degradation of the Arctic. But I am here to tell you otherwise.

The real issue is not and will never be climate change. The real issue is that we have lost part of our humanity. We have lost our capacity to care … . The U.S. may or may not recognize a violation of human rights. But unless we open our hearts and embrace not just people we love, but people we don't know, people we will never meet, and people who are not yet even born, we will never value our species enough to make sure it survives.

– 2 –

Hotel bar. RAPHAËL is behind the bar. JEAN enters.

RAPHAËL

Salut! … Raphaël. At the –

JEAN

Ah oui the new … *T'es devenu barman?*

RAPHAËL

I like to sub once in a while. Keeps things interesting. You're still in town? I thought you were transferring to an ice camp.

JEAN

L'hélicoptère fonctionne pas.

RAPHAËL

Oh.

JEAN

We got new parts delivered yesterday but now the mechanic is sick. *J'peux avoir une bière?*

RAPHAËL hands him a bottle.

RAPHAËL

I can hook you up with some people if you want. I mean, if you're looking for something to do while you're waiting.

JEAN

Non, non, c'est correct. I've got things to do.

RAPHAËL

Oh yeah? What are you working on?

JEAN

Just … measurements. Around here.

RAPHAËL

So you've been out? Did you see the pressure ridge down toward Edgell Island? That thing must be at least twenty feet tall!

JEAN

Non. My uh – My guide doesn't seem inclined to go out.

RAPHAËL

Comment ça?

JEAN

I don't know. Yesterday it was the wind. The day before it was the current. And today the time isn't right. I asked when he expects the time to be right and he couldn't answer. All he could say was "the time isn't right."

RAPHAËL

Maybe he senses that Nuliajuk is angry.

JEAN

Who?

RAPHAËL

The Inuit goddess. You know … With the big hair and the fingerless hands? Apparently when she gets angry –

JEAN looks around.

JEAN

Veronica is not here? I thought she performed every Thursday.

RAPHAËL

You haven't heard?

JEAN

What?

RAPHAËL

Oh man …

JEAN

What?

RAPHAËL

Attends, t'as besoin de quelque chose de plus fort que ça.

He pours a shot for JEAN.

JEAN

What is it?

RAPHAËL

Her son committed suicide.

JEAN reacts.

RAPHAËL

Y a environ une semaine.

JEAN

Chez lui?

RAPHAËL

At a friend's house.

JEAN

Oh God …

RAPHAËL

Nice kid. He used to bum cigarettes from me all the time. I don't smoke but I would buy them anyway just so I could give them to him. (*pause*) *T'as des enfants?*

JEAN

No. Well I almost had a son but he uh – he was stillborn.

RAPHAËL

Oh.

JEAN

At seven months his heart stopped beating. But we did get to hold him for a few minutes.

JEAN downs his shot.

RAPHAËL

Then he knows that you were there. My girlfriend is giving birth at home. We got a midwife to coach me through the process so I can do the delivery myself. If my son is born into my arms, then he'll always know that his father was there.

Beat.

JEAN

How is she doing?

RAPHAËL

Veronica? I think she's pretty devastated.

JEAN

I bet.

RAPHAËL

I was planning on stopping by after my shift. If you want –

JEAN

Non thanks.

RAPHAËL

I'm sure she –

JEAN

Non. It's ... I don't think it's not a good idea.

- 3 -

*Leanna's house. TULUGAQ has fallen asleep
on a chair. VERONICA is huddled in a corner,
expressionless.*

*A spotlight comes on over a microphone. VERONICA
goes to it.*

Beat.

*She opens her mouth to speak ... No sound comes
out. She taps the microphone and tries again.
Nothing.*

*She goes to a wall or a set piece (this can be any
surface suitable for projection) and mouths a few
words. A jumble of letters from the Roman alphabet
appear, dance around for a while, but refuse to settle
into anything resembling language.*

*She moves to a different spot and tries again. This
time, Inuktitut characters appear but the result is
the same.*

*TULUGAQ wakes up. He watches as VERONICA
moves around the stage, desperately trying to
form language. But all she does is leave a trail of
unintelligible blobs.*

LEANNA enters, carrying a suitcase.

LEANNA

Qanuippitik?

Projection (text):
How are you?

VERONICA darts back to her original position and the light over the microphone disappears. LEANNA looks at her.

Beat.

(to TULUGAQ) Sulii sujuqangilaq?

Projection (text):
Still nothing?

He wrinkles his nose.

Nillilaunngilaq?

Projection (text):
Not a word?

TULUGAQ wrinkles his nose.

Niritsianiqsauliqqaa?

Projection (text):
Is she eating more regularly?

TULUGAQ

Tuttuminirmik uujuqtulauqtuq.

Projection (text):
She had caribou stew last night.

LEANNA turns to VERONICA.

LEANNA

Hi, honey …

VERONICA doesn't react.

I'm back … You don't want to talk to me? … I'd love to hear
your voice …

VERONICA doesn't react.

I'm sorry I was gone for so long. I couldn't stop thinking about you.
I tried to change my flight but … you know how it is. There's always
one more meeting, one more person to talk to, one more –

She notices no one is listening.

Well, anyway.

She sits. It's uncomfortable. She gets up again.

How about some tea? I'm dying to have a good cup of tea.
(*to TULUGAQ*) *Tiiturumaviit?*

*TULUGAQ gets up. He goes around and examines
VERONICA's failed attempts at communicating.
LEANNA doesn't see what he sees.*

TULUGAQ

Uqausiit … Titiraqtimut pimmariit.

Projection (text):
Words … Very important for a writer.

LEANNA

Yes, I know –

TULUGAQ

*Uvatsiarutigut, inuuqativut sulijuqsaqtuviniit
uqausiit pimmariugianginnit, silamut
aaqqitaunirmut – anirnikkut, sanngijualukkut. Uqausivut
taimaak aaqqisimammat … Inuunitta, uqausitta
aaqqisimammagu inuusivut..*

Projection (text):

In ancient tradition, our people believed words were
very powerful. Because they were formed with *sila* – the
breath, the great life force. When we speak something, that
something is given substance. It comes into being ... Words
are how our individual will takes shape.

LEANNA

Isumagiatsiakannirialik.

Projection (text):

She needs more time to think ...

TULUGAQ

*Paniit titirasuuq uqausiqarani, mitsirarunniiqtuq. Paniit
silaittukuluujaalirmat.*

Projection (text):

Your daughter is a writer with no words. A will with no
shape. Your daughter seems to have lost some *sila.*

LEANNA *looks at* VERONICA.

- 4 -

Somewhere on the land. MAMA *walks, searching for
something. She is weak and breathes laboriously.*

MAMA

It's somewhere around here, *paniapik* ... I know it is. There's the
bluff. And the river. Somewhere around here ... There was a boulder
on the shore. A boulder shaped like a –

She looks around.

Maybe around this point.

She resumes walking, with great difficulty.

It was up from the river. A cozy cave in a snowdrift. Just big enough for you and me. That's where it all started, *paniapik*. That's where you drew your first breath …

She stifles a sob.

Somewhere around here … A boulder …

She trips.

A boulder shaped like a –

She collapses.

– 5 –

On the ice. A few snowdrifts here and there. JEAN is having a temper tantrum. TULUGAQ stands stoically, his rifle slung over his shoulder.

JEAN

Storm? What storm? *Où ça la tempête?* I don't see any storm look look not a single cloud the sky is perfectly blue!

TULUGAQ

We go back.

JEAN

No we're not going back. The one thing we are not doing is going back. You understand? *On s'en retourne pas!* Every day every single day for the past three weeks there's been a reason not to go out. *Là j'suis tanné.* We're here we have a few more hours of daylight so let's drill some holes and deploy some moorings.

TULUGAQ

I made a mistake. I thought today was right. Today is not right. I can feel.

JEAN

(*exasperated*) You can feel what?

TULUGAQ

Storm.

JEAN

Ben oui c'est ça.

TULUGAQ

And ice is no good.

JEAN

This ice is perfectly fine. (*jumping up and down*) See? I can't believe how hard it is to get anything done around here. I'm going to get the drill.

> He turns to leave. A loud exhale stops him dead in his tracks.

What was that?

> TULUGAQ motions for him to be silent. He raises his rifle. One of the snowdrifts shivers, revealing an unconscious MAMA underneath.

Holy – What's wrong with this bear?

TULUGAQ

You go to the skidoo.

JEAN

It's so emaciated …

TULUGAQ

You pay me to protect you. I say go. You go.

> JEAN moves in a little closer. TULUGAQ rolls his eyes.

JEAN

It doesn't seem injured ...

> *He takes off his mitts and pulls out a water bottle.*
> *In the process, one of the mitts falls on the ice.*

TULUGAQ

I bring flowers and a bottle of wine. You sit and have a nice conversation with *nanuq*.

> *JEAN dribbles water over the bear's mouth. The bear*
> *doesn't react.*

JEAN

Let me try one more time.

> *Again, he dribbles water over MAMA's mouth.*
> *MAMA twitches. TULUGAQ grabs JEAN's arm and*
> *pulls him away.*

TULUGAQ

We go now. If the bear kills you, I have too much paperwork.

JEAN

(*searching his pockets*) Wait. I dropped one of my mitts.

> *He walks back. Just as he bends to pick it up, MAMA*
> *opens her eyes. JEAN freezes. TULUGAQ aims.*

TULUGAQ

Walk back. Slow.

> *JEAN doesn't move. MAMA starts to prop herself up.*

TULUGAQ

Walk back!

> *MAMA growls.*

JEAN

Aaaaaaah!

He takes off.

TULUGAQ and the bear stare at each other.

We hear the ice crack followed by a scream and a splash in the water. TULUGAQ swings around.

TULUGAQ

Fuck.

He goes after JEAN.

Beat.

Something catches MAMA's attention.

MAMA

A boulder shaped like a – (*pause*) There it is, *paniapik*. There it is.

She goes toward it.

– 6 –

Coast Guard centre. RAPHAËL is talking on two different phones.

RAPHAËL

(*to phone 1*) Yeah, they're in Barrow Strait ... The call came in an hour ago ... I don't – wait – (*to phone 2*) POLARIA, YOU STILL THERE? ... What's your position? ... (*to phone 1*) Seventy-four degrees north, ninety-five west ... Fifteen-foot waves and snow falling sideways ...

THOMAS rushes in.

THOMAS

What the hell is going on? Why didn't you call earlier? I leave you in charge for two and a half minutes and –

RAPHAËL

It's really bad.

THOMAS

Bad? You call this bad?

RAPHAËL

The hull is punctured in two places. The captain and a few crew members are trying to launch the life rafts.

THOMAS

It's a fucking disaster is what it is. Do we have a helicopter?

RAPHAËL *indicates to* THOMAS *to hold on.*

RAPHAËL

(*to phone 1*) I'm here … How long is that gonna take? … Yeah, okay. (*to* THOMAS) They have a helicopter. Now they're trying to find a pilot who's willing to fly in this weather. (*to phone 2*) *Polaria*? … HELLO? …

THOMAS

Give me that.

THOMAS *grabs one of the phones.*

(*to phone*) Hi, this is Thomas. Who's this? … Hi, Doug. What's going on? … No, I'll hold … (*to* RAPHAËL) Is the *Terry Fox* nearby?

RAPHAËL

I don't know. (*to phone*) POLARIA? … Oh, I thought I had lost you for a second. What? … Shit …

THOMAS

What happened?

RAPHAËL

(*to THOMAS*) The wind is blowing the rafts away. A few of them tried to jump and they all missed.

THOMAS

Tell them to wait.

RAPHAËL

Tell them to wait? What do you mean tell them to –

THOMAS

(*to phone*) Hey Doug? … I need the line. I'll call you back.

He hangs up and dials again.

(*to RAPHAËL, barking*) KEEP TALKING TO HIM!

RAPHAËL

(*to phone*) Hey man, what's going on out there? … Yeah, we're doing everything we can to – WE'RE DOING EVERYTHING WE CAN TO GET YOU SOME HELP …

THOMAS

(*to phone*) Hi, this is Thomas at the Coast Guard in Iqaluit …

THOMAS makes a gesture indicating to RAPHAËL to keep talking.

RAPHAËL

(*to phone*) WHAT'S YOUR NAME? …

THOMAS

(*to phone*) They called already? Yeah, they just lost several men.

RAPHAËL

(*to phone*) JONAS. I'M RAPHAËL … FROM Montréal … That's right, the French province … How about you? Where are you from?

THOMAS

(*to phone*) Thanks, man. Keep me posted.

He hangs up.

RAPHAËL

(*to phone*) No, I've never been to Munich but I'd love to go some day. There's good hiking around there, right?

THOMAS

(*to RAPHAËL*) The aircraft in Resolute is gonna fly over and drop more rafts.

RAPHAËL

(*to phone*) Yeah, I'm a big hiker … Hey Jonas, my colleague tells me that we have an aircraft on the way … YEAH. THEY'RE GONNA BRING MORE LIFE RAFTS …

The phone rings.

THOMAS

(*to phone*) Coast Guard … Great! Tell him to be careful. I'm looking at the satellite image and it's nasty out there.

He hangs up.

RAPHAËL

They have a pilot?

THOMAS

Yeah.

RAPHAËL

(*to phone*) Hey Jonas? … We've got a rescue helicopter heading – A RESCUE HELICOPTER. YEAH. IS THERE ANYTHING YOU CAN USE TO KEEP WARM?

THOMAS

This is just what we fucking need: a bunch of German scientists dying under our watch.

RAPHAËL

(*to phone*) WHAT? ... (*to THOMAS*) The boat's half-submerged. They're getting hit by waves every thirty seconds.

THOMAS

Tell them to stay together.

RAPHAËL

(*to phone*) YOU GUYS ALL STAY TOGETHER, OKAY? ... (*to THOMAS*) Why is this taking so long?

The phone rings.

THOMAS

(*to phone*) Coast Guard ...

RAPHAËL

(*to phone*) HEY JONAS, ARE YOU MARRIED? ...

THOMAS

(*to phone*) Sorry, Marie, this is a really bad time.

RAPHAËL gestures he wants to take the call.

RAPHAËL

(*to phone*) DO YOU HAVE ANY KIDS?

THOMAS hands him the phone.

THOMAS

(*to RAPHAËL*) Make it quick.

RAPHAËL

(*to Marie on phone*) Allô? ... Non, j'ai oublié. Ça bouge pas mal ici ... Tu pouvais pas dormir? ... Comment ça?

Projection (text):

Hello? ... No, I forgot. There's a lot going on here ... You couldn't sleep? ... How come?

THOMAS

All right, wrap it up.

RAPHAËL indicates he needs one more minute.

RAPHAËL

(*to phone*) WHAT DID YOU SAY, JONAS? (*to phone*) *Marie, attends une seconde.*

Projection (text):
Wait a second, Marie.

(*to phone with Jonas*) YOU CAN HEAR THE PLANE?
(*to THOMAS*) The aircraft's there. (*to phone*) OKAY, JONAS,
THEY'RE GONNA TRY TO DROP THE RAFTS AS
CLOSE TO THE SHIP AS POSSIBLE. (*to phone*) *Marie,
y faut que j'te laisse ... Quoi? ... T'es certaine? ...*

Projection (text):
Marie, I have to go ... What? ... Are you sure? ...

THOMAS

RAPHAËL, GET OFF THE PHONE!

RAPHAËL

(*to phone with Marie*) *Laisse-moi voir ce que j'peux –*

Projection (text):
Let me see what I can –

THOMAS grabs the phone and hangs up.

THOMAS

What's happening?

RAPHAËL

(*to phone*) JONAS, WHAT'S HAPPENING? WHERE ARE
THE RAFTS? ... THE RAFTS? ... NONE OF THEM? ...
(*to THOMAS*) It's too windy. The rafts all blew away and they lost
another five men. Listen, Marie is having –

THOMAS

Then their only chance is the helicopter.

RAPHAËL

(*to Jonas on phone*) I'M SORRY, MAN. YOU'RE GONNA
HAVE TO WAIT FOR THE HELICOPTER ... YEAH.
(*to THOMAS*) Can you take over?

THOMAS

Can I WHAT?

RAPHAËL

Marie is having contractions. I have to –

THOMAS

For fuck's sake, Raphaël. Now's not the time to play daddy.

RAPHAËL

But she might be –

THOMAS

YOU took this call. YOU are the *Polaria*'s lifeline. And when you're
someone's lifeline, you don't get to quit.

RAPHAËL

(*to Jonas on phone*) WHAT? ... YEAH, I'M HERE ... I'm not
going anywhere ... I'm here.

– 7 –

*Deep-blue darkness. Sunlight streams through a hole
in the ice above, illuminating the underwater world.
Muffled voices create a tapestry of plaintive sounds.*

*JEAN, seemingly unconscious, is being rocked back
and forth by a gentle tidal movement. The same
long strands that appeared earlier float around him.
A strand brushes his face.*

JEAN comes to with a start.

He looks around, lost. The water turns his movements into a kind of weightless ballet.

NULIAJUK

(*whispering*) Who. Are. You.

JEAN

Allô?

NULIAJUK

(*louder*) Who. Are. You.

JEAN

Liz?

A youthful giggle reverberates throughout the liquid world.

Liz, c'est toi?

A shift in the light reveals larger-than-life NULIAJUK. The plant-like strands are part of her wild mane. Various SEA ANIMALS, including the DAUGHTER bear, are trapped in it.

Whoa ... That's ... That's a lot of hair.

She giggles again.

NULIAJUK

They call me. Kanna.

> *Projection (text):*
> This One Below.

They call me. Samani.

Projection (text):
Out at Sea.

They call me. Sanna.

Projection (text):
Down There.

But I am Nuliajuk.
Inuit Goddess. Of the Ocean.
And the Underworld.

JEAN

Oh it's funny you sound exactly like my wife. Well my
ex-wife ... Wait. Did you say goddess?

NULIAJUK

You. Like my father.
Weak.
Makes me.
Very very.
Cranky.

JEAN

Oh my God.

NULIAJUK

He.
Cut off. My fingers.

JEAN

I'm losing my mind.

NULIAJUK

Let fear.
Guide his heart.

> *JEAN looks up toward the light, evaluating his
> chances of making it to the surface.*

JEAN

> (*to himself*) *Okay calme reste calme* ... Cognitive
> disturbances ... decreased motor control ... I'm not dead this is
> just cerebral hypoxia – not enough oxygen going to the brain.

> *He gathers his strength and tries to push himself up
> but the* SEA ANIMALS *grab him.*

SEA ANIMALS

> (*whispering*) Help me ...

JEAN

> What – No. Don't –

> *He struggles to free himself.*

SEA ANIMALS

> (*whispering*) Help me ... Help me ...

> NULIAJUK *wraps strands of her hair around him.*

JEAN

> No. Let me go. LET ME GO!

NULIAJUK

> Jean.

JEAN

> How do you know my name?

NULIAJUK

> Bird-spirit wanted. To take me away.
> My father's power rose.
> To fight. Bird-spirit.
> Spirit shaken.
> Briefly.
> Then spirit's power grew.
> Dark.
> Heavy.

Overwhelming.
My father.
Threw me.
Overboard.
Threw me.
Into the icy water.
I gripped. The kayak.
Cut off. My fingers.
One two three four five six seven eight nine ten.
With his knife.

JEAN

That's – I'm sorry that's terrible but –

NULIAJUK

Here.
At the bottom. Of the sea.
I was reborn.
Now the ocean. Is my dominion.
Here.
I can sense. The weakness.
Of all.
Humanity.

JEAN

But what does any of this have to do with –

NULIAJUK

WEAK!

*Her anger triggers a cacophony of frightened
SEA ANIMAL responses.*

Let fear.
Guide your heart.

*NULIAJUK wraps more hair around JEAN,
immobilizing him.*

JEAN

No don't please that's ... Aaaah ... Look you seem like a very nice
young woman –

NULIAJUK

Cranky.

JEAN

Yeah that too *mais pour de bonnes raisons*. And I'm all for – I'm all
for working it out you know 'cause life is a beautiful thing and I'd like
to enjoy as much of mine as I can so if there's anything –

> *NULIAJUK has created a dark hair cocoon around*
> *JEAN that completely traps him.*

NULIAJUK

Like my father.
Don't protect me.
At a time. When.
I need it most.

JEAN

Then I will I'll protect you I promise. I'll do anything you want
me to do ...

NULIAJUK

Prove.

JEAN

Prove? Prove how? I mean I – I –

NULIAJUK

AAAAAAAAAAARGH!!!

JEAN

I will! I'll prove it to you I'll –

NULIAJUK

Weak.

JEAN

No please ... Noooooooooo!

DAUGHTER & SEA ANIMALS

Help me ... Help me ...

> *The phrase echoes endlessly while JEAN is swallowed into the cocoon and everything recedes into a dark blue mystery.*

– 8 –

> *Leanna's house. VERONICA is still huddled in a corner, expressionless. LEANNA sits facing her.*

LEANNA

The weather has been weird all month. One day we're walking around in T-shirts, the next day it's snowing. (*pause*) It feels like the whole world is out of whack. (*pause*) *Takuqqaujara Inuujaq ullaaq.* She and the other students at school miss you. She asked me to give you this drawing.

> *LEANNA shows a drawing of Samuel flying over an arctic landscape.*

She says Samuel's *anirniq* has gone back to *sila.*

> *She stares at VERONICA, waiting for her to react.*

Veronica, say something! I'm here! That's what you wanted, isn't it? I've cancelled everything, the least you can do is speak to me! (*pause*) *Awh, taima.* We didn't survive for four thousand years by throwing in the towel every time we encounter hardship. It's hard? Yes, it's hard. Now get up on your feet and fight. *Tusaavingaa?* Get up!

> *She grabs VERONICA and tries to get her up on her feet.*

Makilirit!

> VERONICA *struggles to free herself.* LEANNA
> *doesn't let go. The two women fight silently until*
> VERONICA *pushes her mother and finds refuge in*
> *another corner of the room.*

What do you want? What do you want me to tell you? That I'm
sorry? That I should have done things differently? That I failed you
and Samuel as a mother and a grandmother? Is that what you want?

> *A long silence.* LEANNA's *tough shell starts to crack.*

Paniapik, ajuinnaqqagit ... Don't leave me alone with this.

– 9 –

> *Coast Guard centre.* RAPHAËL *is still on the phone.*
> THOMAS *is on the* VHF *radio.*

THOMAS

(*to radio*) Do you see the ship?

RAPHAËL

(*to phone*) CAN YOU SEE THE HELICOPTER? ...
(*to* THOMAS) He can hear it.

THOMAS

(*to* RAPHAËL) Can he give us any kind of position?

RAPHAËL

(*to phone*) CAN YOU TELL WHERE
THE – JONAS? ... JONAS? ... CAN YOU TELL WHERE
THE HELICOPTER IS IN RELATION TO YOU? ...
(*to* THOMAS) I can barely hear him.

THOMAS

   (*to RAPHAËL*) The pilot's gonna try to go lower.

RAPHAËL

   (*to phone*) CAN YOU SEE IT NOW? (*to THOMAS*)
   They can see it!

THOMAS

   (*to RAPHAËL*) Are there only three of them?

RAPHAËL

   (*to phone*) HOW MANY ARE YOU, JONAS? ...
   (*to THOMAS*) Yeah, only three.

THOMAS

   (*to RAPHAËL*) They're lowering the ladder.

RAPHAËL

   (*to phone*) JONAS, LISTEN TO ME. THIS IS YOUR
   CHANCE. YOU GOTTA GET ON THAT LADDER, YOU
   HEAR ME? THINK ABOUT YOUR WIFE. THINK ABOUT
   ALL THE GOOD HIKING PLACES YOU HAVEN'T –
   WHAT? ... (*to THOMAS*) The ladder's out of reach.

THOMAS

   (*to radio*) They can't reach it, can you move in closer? ...
   (*to RAPHAËL*) He's being whipped around by the wind. He's
   gonna circle around and try again.

RAPHAËL

   (*to phone*) OKAY, JONAS, GET READY. THE PILOT'S
   GONNA CIRCLE AROUND AND – (*listening*) NO,
   CIRCLE AROUND ...

THOMAS

   (*to RAPHAËL*) He's coming back.

RAPHAËL

(*to phone*) WHAT? ... (*to THOMAS*) He's gonna let the other two go up first.

Tense beat.

THOMAS

(*to radio*) You got one? (*to RAPHAËL*) They've got one! (*to radio*) Congratulations!

RAPHAËL

Woo-hoo!

They high-five each other.

THOMAS

(*to radio*) All right, two more to go.

RAPHAËL

(*to phone*) JONAS? ... HEY MAN, I'M COUNTING ON YOU, OKAY? I'M GONNA BE WAITING HERE WITH A CUP OF COFFEE ... NO, COME ON ... I KNOW BUT I SWEAR, IT WON'T BE NECESSARY ... ALL RIGHT, WHAT'S HER NAME? ... Hannah. YES, I WILL TELL HER.

THOMAS

(*to RAPHAËL*) The other one's up.

RAPHAËL

(*to phone*) ALL RIGHT, JONAS. I KNOW YOUR HANDS ARE FROZEN BUT YOU GOTTA DO THIS, MAN. JUST LIKE THE OTHER TWO.

THOMAS

(*to RAPHAËL*) Okay, he's gotta go now.

RAPHAËL

(*to phone*) YES, I WROTE IT DOWN. HANNAH ...

THOMAS
(*to RAPHAËL*) NOW!

RAPHAËL
(*to THOMAS*) He's going up ...

RAPHAËL puts the phone down.

THOMAS
(*to radio*) Okay, this is your last one ...

Long, excruciating beat.

RAPHAËL
Come on, Jonas. Come on, Jonas. You can do it. You can
fucking do it ...

THOMAS
(*to RAPHAËL*) He's on the ladder.

RAPHAËL
Come on, Jonas ...

THOMAS looks at RAPHAËL. He shakes his head no.

FUCK!

He slams the phone.

Fuck, fuck, FUCK!

*He thrashes around, punching the walls and kicking
everything.*

THOMAS
(*to radio*) Thanks, man ... Yeah, get home safe.

RAPHAËL
Jonas, you fucking FUCK! All you had to do was hold on to the
fucking ladder!

THOMAS

Raphaël, you're gonna hurt yourself.

RAPHAËL

All he had to do was hold on!

THOMAS

I know.

RAPHAËL

How fucking hard is that?

THOMAS

I'm sure he tried.

RAPHAËL

Jonas, Jonas, Jonas ...

THOMAS

Come on. Sit down.

RAPHAËL

We were gonna go hiking together.

The phone rings.

THOMAS

(*to phone*) Coast Guard ... Hold on ...

He hands the phone to RAPHAËL, *who doesn't take
it.* THOMAS *insists.*

RAPHAËL

Hello? ... Yeah, this is Raphaël ... Oh my God ...

Tears stream down his face.

(*to* THOMAS) I'm a dad.

Tulugaq's house. JEAN is propped up in bed, drinking hot tea. TULUGAQ sits with him.

TULUGAQ

You combed her hair?

JEAN

Did I comb her hair?

TULUGAQ

Yes.

JEAN

No I did not comb her hair.

TULUGAQ

You have to comb her hair.

JEAN

Well I'm sorry I didn't have a comb handy.

TULUGAQ

Nuliajuk is very angry. If you don't comb her hair, she keeps all the sea animals away from hunters. Hunters have no food. You have to comb her hair so she feels love.

JEAN

It's a little late for that.

TULUGAQ

Go back.

JEAN

You want me to jump back into the Arctic Ocean?

TULUGAQ

I am a hunter. I cannot work with you if Nuliajuk is angry.

JEAN

I was unconscious I – there was no one in the water …

TULUGAQ

You saw.

JEAN

A lot of people see things when they come close to death. It's the brain firing off you know … it was my imagination going crazy.

TULUGAQ

If you believe, it is real. If you don't believe, it is not real.

JEAN

You believe it was real?

TULUGAQ

I believe I see Nuliajuk, I comb her hair.

    Beat.

JEAN

What was she trying to escape? When her father cut off her fingers?

TULUGAQ

Nuliajuk is a stubborn girl. She doesn't want to marry. Father says: you must marry. Nuliajuk marries a young man. Beautiful. Kind. Young man takes her away to live on his island. But young man is not a young man. Young man is a bird-spirit.

JEAN

Oh.

TULUGAQ

Evil spirit. Nuliajuk has many tears. One day, her father comes to visit. She tells him about bird-spirit. Father tries to bring Nuliajuk back home in his *qajak*. Bird-spirit attacks. Father is scared. He throws Nuliajuk in the water.

JEAN

Shouldn't her father comb her hair then?

TULUGAQ

Nuliajuk didn't ask her father. She asked you.

JEAN

Pourquoi moi?

TULUGAQ

I don't know. Only you can answer.

Beat.

More tea?

JEAN

No I'm fine.

TULUGAQ

You have some colour in your face. You're better now.

JEAN

Yeah I feel better. Thank you.

TULUGAQ

Okay. But I don't work with you anymore. I don't work with you until you comb Nuliajuk's hair.

- 11 -

Leanna's house. VERONICA is awake but motionless, as if frozen in place. LEANNA and JEAN enter.

LEANNA

Veronica, honey ... Jean came to see you ... You don't want to talk to him?

VERONICA doesn't react.

JEAN

I'd love to hear your poetry …

VERONICA doesn't react.

JEAN

And learn more Inuktitut … *J'ai* uh I did figure out what *pitsiaqattautiniq* means. (*to LEANNA*) Am I saying it right?

LEANNA

Close enough.

JEAN

(*to VERONICA*) It means respect. See, for a *qallunaaq*, I'm not that clueless.

VERONICA doesn't react.

JEAN

(*to LEANNA*) How long has it been?

LEANNA

Weeks. I don't know what to do anymore.

> *JEAN pulls something wrapped in cloth from his pocket. He unwraps it. It is Tulugaq's polar bear sculpture.*

JEAN

I uh … This is for you.

> *He puts it on VERONICA's lap.*

I thought it could keep you company.

LEANNA

Thank you.

JEAN

After my son – (*pause*) It took a long time. It takes a long time.

LEANNA

I know.

JEAN

We lost him shortly after I gave a keynote. It was in Houston Texas –
hot as hell. Some blogger didn't like my views about a possible
carbon tax and posted me and my wife's email address online.
We started receiving death threats. I wasn't too concerned – some
of my colleagues had been threatened before – but Liz got scared.
She uh … she wanted to go to the police. I thought that was a bad
idea. I didn't want to look like a … you know. A few days later some
lunatic walked up to her and started threatening her. I don't think it
went on for very long – there were other people nearby so someone
called the police – but she was very shaken. That night she uh … we
were lying in bed and she said … she told me something was
wrong. We went to the hospital. They confirmed the baby's heart
had stopped beating.

LEANNA

That must have been very hard.

JEAN

I didn't protect her.

LEANNA

Maybe you were just looking in the wrong direction. It's very easy to
do that. Very easy.

  Beat.

When are you going back?

JEAN

À la fin de la semaine. The helicopter is finally working but the
storm ripped the multi-year ice off the coast. It's now drifting down
Davis Strait. We totally missed it …

LEANNA

The appeal was denied.

JEAN

    I'm sorry.

LEANNA

    I guess it was to be expected.

JEAN

    You know … Maybe we should figure out a way to join forces.
    If I knew I could put the data to good use I might consider taking
    that contract.

LEANNA

    Let me finish my job here first. But maybe when things get better …

       They reach for each other's hand.

    Thank you for stopping by.

       He starts to leave then stops.

JEAN

    I uh … I know this is gonna sound weird but – Do you
    have a comb?

LEANNA

    A comb?

JEAN

    Yeah.

       She exits and comes back with a comb. JEAN
       approaches VERONICA. *She recoils.*

    Let me …

       He moves toward her again and starts combing her hair.

       Beat.

       JEAN *invites* LEANNA *to take over. She hesitates.*
       He places her hand on top of his.

Together, they comb VERONICA's *hair.* VERONICA's
*eyes well up with tears ... and she finally allows herself
to sob.*

(For music here, try "Sila" by Tanya Tagaq.)

*Voices rise all around them, happy and light, like
when school lets out for recess. The light shifts to reveal*
NULIAJUK's *hair loosening and releasing the trapped
animals. Before they swim away, they gather in one of
those unexpected formations only Nature knows how
to create, and celebrate life with a water ballet.*

DAUGHTER *bear waits for her turn ... then soon,
she is released too. She joins in the celebration ... but
something is tugging at her and she must leave. She
swims up ... and up ... with the grace and energy of
youth but when she reaches the surface, she doesn't
stop, she keeps going, up into the sky and beyond, up,
up, becoming a flying bear, becoming a spirit.*

DAUGHTER

    I'm coming, Anaana!

− 12 −

An official ceremony. THOMAS *and* RAPHAËL,
*looking sharp in their Coast Guard uniforms, stand
at attention. They speak in a low voice while the
unseen ceremony unfolds.*

THOMAS

    Have you picked a name yet?

RAPHAËL

    We have.

THOMAS

What is it?

RAPHAËL

I'm not telling. We won't decide for sure until I meet him.

THOMAS

Come on, tell me.

RAPHAËL

No, you have to wait like everyone else.

THOMAS

I hope it's not Raphaël.

RAPHAËL

Shut up.

THOMAS

Raphaëls are wimps.

RAPHAËL

Oh, and Thomases are better?

THOMAS

Much.

> *Beat.*

> *They smile and nod to an unseen dignitary.*

RAPHAËL

If we call him Thomas, the poor thing will turn into an asshole before he has time to say his first word.

> *THOMAS play-slaps RAPHAËL on the back of the head.*

Hey! What the –

THOMAS

Shhh ... Official visit. Behave yourself.

RAPHAËL

You behave yourself.

They turn their attention to the ceremony.

RAPHAËL

Did you manage to set up a meeting with the P.M.?

THOMAS

Nope. His assistant said we're better off lying low until the whole
Polaria-debacle-slash-public-relations nightmare has blown over.

RAPHAËL

So ... no port?

THOMAS

There will be a port. But it won't be built under my watch. And
you know, all things considered, maybe that's not such a bad thing.
(*pause*) Could be I need to make room for the next generation.

RAPHAËL

How altruistic of you.

THOMAS

Careful.

RAPHAËL

You said it first.

THOMAS

I'm still your superior.

RAPHAËL

Not for long.

THOMAS suddenly shifts his attention.

THOMAS

Shhh. Here's the P.M.

They salute as the Prime Minister walks by.

THOMAS

He's a little guy.

RAPHAËL

With the charisma of a roadkill.

THOMAS

Yeah well, we had to leave something for the Americans.

The Canadian anthem starts to play in the background. They listen for a while.

RAPHAËL

So this is it, huh? You're gonna be a retiree?

THOMAS

Apparently.

RAPHAËL

You know, they should rename the Road to Nowhere after you. It's rough, full of potholes, and it looks like its only purpose is to take you to a pit but, if you know where to look, it does have its qualities.

THOMAS

I did my best, Raphaël. Granted, it wasn't much but it was my best. Now it's up to you.

RAPHAËL

Geez, thanks.

THOMAS

You take good care of this place.

RAPHAËL

I will.

VERONICA, at the microphone. She performs a
spoken-word poem.

VERONICA

no sleep for the Wicked
ain't right
no sleep for the Haunted
more like
we've got but this
one life
how many thousand nights
be no man left standing
be no woman left standing
nobody be handing
us our plate our silver spoon
we're born and gone too soon
up the moon rise up the tide rise
up to blue skies
and up to heaven we hope
we hope in our brown eyes
we hope down to our brown toes
fortune come and she goes
she come and she goes
she come and she goes

All characters (except MAMA and her DAUGHTER)
appear one by one and watch VERONICA perform.

and we're still packing, tracking
feet on path – not so straight
not so narrow, still not lacking for
sweet things, peaches, river beaches
and rocky shores
we can take much and
Lord give us more
Lord give us more
Lord give us more

this is a high waved sea
the bay is a live
deep breathing thing

deep grieving, wring
our hands for days past
ring the bell for loved ones passed
scooped up babies

MAMA appears.

maybe we stood in dark doorways
maybe we died in back hallways
maybe lost in storm
maybe slipped through crack
in ice, in alley

DAUGHTER

Anaanaa!

MAMA searches for her DAUGHTER.

VERONICA

maybe we walk the shadowed valley
or climb up on ridge
high up on bridge
inclined to jump – but wait
while yet we breathe
it's never too late
so they say

are we preyed upon let us pray
not, neither by foe neither by friend
maybe we're prosperous blessed
big shot hot topic
rocket top hit of the century
got baby got sweets got
house got wheels got
threads hot treads
and money in the bank
maybe we pull rank
on minions, amass millions
maybe we rage maybe we fight
politicking day and night
out the wrong for right
hold up torch till end
sew up wounds and mend

string up demons and send
way way way

The DAUGHTER appears, hovering in the air.

DAUGHTER

I'm here …

VERONICA

cherish our fast done days

*MAMA reaches for her DAUGHTER. She cannot touch
her but feels her presence.*

DAUGHTER

I'm here, Anaana. In the clouds, in the mountains, in the snow, in the
ice. I'm here. I'm here …

*After a moment the DAUGHTER drifts away. MAMA lets
her go.*

VERONICA

no no no we can't stay
we can't stay
nor for fame
nor for glory
still I'm told
it's a gift
end of story

They all take a deep breath in …

Projection (text):
Listen.
I am right here.
Inside of you.
… and let it out.

Blackout.

– END OF PLAY –

ACKNOWLEDGEMENTS

I am extremely grateful to everyone who shared their expertise and patiently answered questions during my research for this play: Leanna Ellsworth at the Inuit Circumpolar Council; Jean-Pierre Lehnert at the Iqaluit Marine Communications and Traffic Services; Jamal Shirley at the Nunavut Research Institute; biologist Thomas Doniol-Valcroze; climate scientists Kerry Emmanuel, Melanie Fitzpatrick, Shari Gearheard, Gavin Schmidt, and Bruno Tremblay; and Inuit climate change activist Sheila Watt-Cloutier.

Sila went through an extensive development process that included residencies, workshops with actors and directors, and public presentations. I am indebted to many organizations and individuals without whom this invaluable work would not have been possible. Among them, I would like to extend a special thanks to Michael Bradford, Downing Cless, Deborah Kinghorn, Theresa May, Saimata Manning, Matt McGeachy, Taqralik Partridge, Megan Sandberg-Zakian, Seema Sueko, Emma Tibaldo, Nigel Williams, Debra Wise, and Jose Zayas.

I also want to thank my agent Beth Blickers for her friendship and her help, as well as scholar Janet Tamalik McGrath, and Talonbooks editor Ann-Marie Metten, who both provided smart and kind advice on the intricacies of the Inuktitut and English languages.

Finally, my deepest respect and gratitude go to the people of Baffin Island who welcomed me with warmth, and agreed to share their stories with me.

CHANTAL BILODEAU

Chantal Bilodeau is a New York–based playwright and translator originally from Montréal. She serves as the artistic director of The Arctic Cycle – an organization created to support the writing of eight plays about the impact of climate change on the eight countries in the Arctic – and is the founder of the blog *Artists and Climate Change*. Her plays have been produced or developed at theatres and universities in the United States, Canada, Mexico, Italy, and Norway, and presented at sustainability, policy, and scientific conferences. She was awarded the Woodward International Playwriting Prize, and First Prize in the Earth Matters on Stage Ecodrama Festival and the Uprising National Playwriting Competition. She is the recipient of a Jerome Travel and Study Grant and a National Endowment for the Arts Fellowship, and has been in residence at Yaddo, MacDowell, the Banff Centre, and the National Theatre School of Canada.